Behind Dark Waters

Pramila Venkateswaran

Plain View Press
P. O. 42255
Austin, TX 78704

plainviewpress.net
sb@plainviewpress.net
1-512-441-2452

Copyright Pramila Venkateswaran, 2008. All rights reserved.
ISBN: 978-0-911051-36-0
Library of Congress Number: 2008941719

Cover Art: "Woman," by Jayashree George. Photographed by Guy Wulfing.

Acknowledgements

Acknowledgements are made to the following publications in which these poems have appeared, a few in different versions or titles:

"Praying for Miracles at Velankani Amman's Shrine, Tamil Nadu" *After Shocks: The Poetry of Recovery*; "America's Collateral Damage" *And Then*; "You Don't Mind My Asking About Death, Do You?" and "Unholy Laws" *en(Compass)*; "Dancer" and "Post-Genesis Love" *Iodine Poetry Journal*; "Rhyme with Me" *Kavya Bharati*; "Me, Mama" *Literary Review*; "Lake Woman" and "Lullaby" *Long Island Sounds Anthology*, 2007; "The Logic of Water," "Paradise in My Palm" and "After a Guest's Departure" *Long Island Quarterly*; "Women Like Us," "Woman Poet," and "Dilli ka Laddoo" *Nassau Review*; "Mother's Weapon" and "Fragments of the Aftermath" *Oberon*; "Night Vision" *Paumanok: Poetry and Pictures of Long Island*; "Diminuendo" *Prairie Schooner*; "Cartographer of the Breast" and "Grandmother's Bedside" *Songs of Seasoned Women*; "My Body" *South Asian Review*; "Nude" *The Light of City and Sea*; "Hunger Vigil" *The Politics of Water* (special issue of *International Feminist Journal of Politics*, Vol. 9); "Mary at Chartres Cathedral" and "Où habitez-vous" *Wednesdays at Curley's*; "A Planet of Women" *Women's Studies Quarterly*, Fall 2007; "Draupadi's Dharma" *Writing the Lines of our Hands*; "Mad Women of Tenkasi," "I Plant a Flag on my Tongue," "Cochin Tale" and "A Planet of Women" *museindia.com*; "Vigil" *freelori.org*; "Women Waiting" *Xanadu*.

I am grateful to Hedgebrook and Norcroft women writers' colonies for awarding me residencies during the summers of 2002 and 2003, which enabled me to write many of the poems in this volume.

Thanks to Ralph Nazareth, Ginger Williams, and Carolyn Emerson for their encouragement and support.

I am indebted to my sister, Jayashree, for choreographing dances to a few of my poems and performing them at the American Art Therapy Association and Washington State Psychology Association conferences.

Contents

Warrior's Chant   9

    Warrior's Chant   11
    Krishna's Reply to Arjuna   13
    our little lives   14
    Vigil   15
    Praying for Miracles at Velankani Amman's Shrine,
    Tamil Nadu   16
    Sita's Song   17

Draupadi's Dharma   19

    Someday I'll Write My Story   21
    A Sound's Body   22
    Mad Women of Tenkasi   23
    Burkha-Bikini   27
    The Stuff of Scheherezade   30
    Woman Poet   32
    Draupadi's Dharma   33
    Cartographer of the Breast   35
    Hunger Vigil   36
    America's Collateral Damage   38
    June Song   39

The Logic of Water   41

    Post-Genesis Love   43
    The Logic of Water   44
    I Plant a Flag on My Tongue   46
    Upping the Ante   48
    Unholy Laws   49
    Women Waiting   50
    Ghosts in My Ears   51
    Cochin Tale   53
    Diminuendo   54
    First Bra Story   55
    Walls   56

Killer Bees	57
Thin	58
My Body	59
Children of War	60
Lullaby	62
Uncle's Letter to Father, 1980	64
Dilli Ka Laddoo	65
Rhyme With Me	66

Women Like Us   67

Fragments of the Aftermath	69
Peace	71
Mary at Chartres Cathedral	72
Où habitez-vous?	73
Nude	74
Sex Contract	77
The Escort	78
A Planet of Women	79
Dancer	82
Mother's Weapon	83
Listening to a Poet at The Frost Place, 1999	84
Grandmother's Bedside	85
Kaikeyi to Her Husband	86
Night Vision	87
Paradise in My Palm	88
After a Guest's Departure	89
You Don't Mind My Asking About Death, Do You?	90
Women Like Us	91
Mother's Holidays	93
Me, Mama	94
Lake Woman	95
Ghazal	96
Notes	97
About the Author	99

" 'Blessed woman! Won't you listen to my words?'

And Kannaki, her face shriveled with pain,
Turned to her right and asked:
                        'Who are you
Following me? Can you fathom the depth
Of my sorrow?'"
            The Tale of an Anklet,
            The Chillapatikaram of Ilanko Atikal
            Translated by R. Parthasarathy

"The simplest part of this poem
is the truth in each one of us
to which it is speaking."

            Audre Lorde, *Undersong*

Warrior's Chant

Warrior's Chant

Do not count the hours:

Suppress the hardness rising up in your throat.

Breathe.

Pick up the task where you left off, blow the dust away
        to see the world.

Engage every muscle of your soul to layer your void –
        light, color, wings.

Will your thoughts to the elements,
        your words their animators.

Believe what-is-a-woman-supposed-to-do question flowered
        at your past funeral:

In recent lives it has become chaff
        in the palm of your hand.

Look wild; you are full of the un-maya, the light
        in the far reaches holding you up.

Wrest your image from the-wife-of, sharpen your trident,
> tuck your sari edge into your waist,

Adjust your seat on the lion's brilliant spine,
> readying for the fight.

Krishna's Reply to Arjuna

Krishna, do wars make sense?
Why fight against my own kin?
Krishna, restore my balance!

Arjuna, have you slept through my lectures?
For you are still at the beginning,
asking if wars make sense.

Look at war with a spiritual lens.
Do warriors think of me often
to restore their balance?

Among their mind's inhabitants
am I number one?
Only then ask if wars make sense.

Am I more than a passing glance?
More than the stars that blink
to restore the traveler's balance?

I am the woman who held the infant,
also the man who held the AK-47,
so, certainly, wars don't make sense
if I am absent to restore balance.

our little lives

you wonder how one lives after horror

but we do

as if something old inhabits us
and we have done this before
picking up where we left off

without hope, without dreams
to simply dwell in the gap
between opposites

as a little girl in the hub of bloody hands
or the one in a crossfire
in an antiseptic city

each picks up her little life
and walks toward some uncertain
sun

Vigil

    for Lori Berenson

even under the most crushing state machinery courage rises up again and again...
        Aung San Suu Kyi, *Freedom from Fear*

Our candles flicker in December wind, shaping letters
to you in your mountain cell, and to others crouching
in cold lit by imagined day, waiting to hold a familiar hand;
we, too, touch emptiness, tall and wide as a stone's inside.

Cupping palms over evasive flame, we walk to the quad,
sheltered from a world reflected in absurd mirrors,
where up is down and wrong is right, where vision is clouded,
ears wax, and memory sheds its skin
quicker than the plop of a stone dropped in a drying well.

We write in flame to aging lives fighting for dreams
wild as this light threatened by winter gusts,
while you summon day in your night,
strum scales, count calluses, mementos of grim growth,
anything to remember, before silence closes our page.

Praying for Miracles at Velankani Amman's Shrine, Tamil Nadu

I stand with mother in a weary line winding through
a dusty courtyard into the church doorway,
my right fist tightening around a one-inch brass
foot I picked out from masses of metal organs
displayed in slotted tin trays. Knee problem,
murmurs a graying woman, wiping perspiration
from her face with the end of her sari, a joint
shining in her palm. *Velankani amman, take care of me,*
each utters, under the cool roof of the steeple,
dropping messages with chosen limbs or organs
into a box at the altar's foot. Hands folded,
we kneel on the cool floor, spires of prayers
rising from our mouths to mingle with the incense.
Our eyes drink in the Virgin's blessing. Outside,
crows from mango pews caw ceaselessly.
The pain in my foot nags like their tireless cry.
I meet Velankani Mary's tranquil gaze above
the pleats of her garment, each like the fold
in my left foot where stitches forced skin and skin to mesh.
I look at the brass in my palm, neat and whole,
unlike the ravine with a twisting stream in my foot.
If the marring of my flesh brings me here,
then this is how a goddess stitches me to her.

Sita's Song

I viewed Sita, goes this Tamil song
translating the devotee's glance into song.

While *saw* is a verb for the ordinary,
viewed describes his yearning as song.

As if he has sighted a planetary body,
his emotions swell into song.

To hear these words must set Rama free,
as it does me when I glimpse Sita in this song.

She is silent as this spring raga rises to "ri"
thrilling pentatonic, unfolding into song.

As the melody wavers in the Lanka valley
will this wife and mother break out of the song?

Language places her in wonderful proximity,
but will the singer speak Sita's desire in his song?

Poet, why make Rama the center of your story,
when Pramila's Sita's heart is breaking into song?

Draupadi's Dharma

Someday I'll Write My Story

I'll write I married, had kids, cooked,
dressed up to bargain at the fish market on Sundays,
quarreled with my mother-in-law, attended mass,
never looked at men because they had sex in their eyes.

I told him one day I'm tired of carrying your weight,
I burn for books.

I'll write about the night
when my body shook like leaves in a storm,
my arms clamped around me to make it stop,
my tongue sputtered Our Father till I went mad,
and grew still only when light crept in.

There's so much to tell, I don't know where to begin,
from my birth when my fate was written
with a bad hand, how to explain the weird bends,
or when I plunged my hands
into life, submerging old routes.

I'll write about walking Maria
to the clinic, travel papers tucked into my slip,
crisp, the stamp on them like a stain.

How a woman stepped out of me,
flew to New York, sipping ginger ale,
her home, a green dot on the Caribbean,
how she dropped her ring into a manhole
on Lexington, by the zebra crossing.

A Sound's Body

> *Women's writings become nourricriture, a "linguistic flesh"*
>   Trinh Min-ha

In Arabic, woman and wound
have the same sound   depending
on context one gauges its meaning
Assia Djebar writes

But how different does a woman's context get
in each language
when it becomes her dress

Like in Tamil *ponnu* girl and *punnu* wound
flesh word   word flesh
are separated by a vowel change

if your lips strained deeper to shape a round cave
girl is a suppurating wound
cast so by a plot of vowels and consonants

I say *ponnu-punnu*   girl wound
and search for its companion in English
off-internal rhyme and homonym

I see woman flesh out woeman
witness a sign's power over our experience

near identical twins
wearing the same suit of woe

Mad Women of Tenkasi

1

Carol, Jay, and I enter the men's side of the fall,
above the mountain goddess' shrine,
aware of a hundred eyes accusing us of transgressing
the gender divide at the waterfall – fierce waters
for men and gentler falls for women.
Water thunders down, giant, white slabs
that could split our heads.

Wills warm, we step into the storm:
eyes half shut, hands on guard rails,
our feet rooted beside the men,
shirts sticking to our skins,
hair pulled back from our puckered faces.

Mother, fully dressed, stands by our pile of dry
clothes wondering why we wanted so badly
to experience the men's waterfall.
Wasn't the less outrageous enough?
Didn't we mind men staring
at our breasts and thighs wet clothes accentuate?

As her thoughts dart between naked men
floating in a pool nearby and us inching into madness,
we dig our heels into stubborn ground, our toes
curving to hold mossy rock as we brave wilder waters
plunging into a whipped cloud cauldron,
our breaths, short puffs, our necks exposed
to the incessant hammering.

2

In Tenkasi, women from nearby insane asylums
are brought to stand under the ferocious falls
in the hope that the icy shock will cure them.
I tuck away this fact in my bulging data
on cures for madness in women.

One busload after another, the women, men
and children line up behind yellow ropes
snaking their way to the rocks – the insane
and the sane. I can't tell the difference
in their wonder and eagerness as they
push forward, until a mass of bodies huddles
tightly under a full stream rushing its green
abundance onto the screaming humanity.

One slip and it's perdition, but clutching limbs,
rope and energy of joined desire
keep our footholds firm, until ordered
to make room for the next busload.

And so on and on, on one side the women
give themselves to the water's will,
the men on the other, stoic except
for the first shiver, violence of water
on rock their antidote.

3

Amani of Tenkasi became a myth when she
behaved like she owned her body.

One morning women doing their laundry
by the river look up to see her wedding necklace
with its sacred talismans
arc through the air and into the stream.

Amani watches the current swallow
the snake of thread, as if accepting
her divorce.

Rivers accept
any offering indifferently.
She adjusts her sari around her shoulders,
clambers up the mossy bank,

then heads home.

4

I kiss the sudden Tenkasi wind
wafting through grandfather's home.

I imagine the antiseptic smell
from his room vying
with tamarind and coriander.
Grandmother comes back with the kids
after a day at the waterfall,
hangs their wet clothes on the line
and begins dinner.

Later the family gathers on the porch
to watch the gods taken on a ride
in a palanquin, devotees serenading
them down the road and into
the sanctum in time for their nap.

I feel this family's presence as I pick
out old dolls from grandmother's trunk
and line them up to be cleaned, painted
and packed away to be displayed

in my glass cabinet in New York –
a fat heifer, two merchants selling fruit,
Krishna with milkmaids,
Shiva dancing on a demon, and Hanuman,
plump-cheeked and humble.

How she meticulously guarded them
through four generations while
the living fragmented! Grandfather,
paralyzed with sorrow at his daughter's
leaving, dies broken, the sons become
patriarchs and mother does their bidding.

I close the emptied trunk.
A fine white spray rises to my face.

Burkha-Bikini

You are so many yards of material,
sometimes shiny black, often opaque, dull;
don't you feel best when you simply lie
in a heap in the corner rather than cover bodies
for hours and sicken in their sticky sweat?

> *I don't need your pity, my pretty friend!*
> *I worry about you barely there. Your ontology*
> *is a question that leads me to wonder about*
> *the morality of the women you seek to serve.*

Hey, hey, hey! Let's take it one at a time.
First, my ontology is quite fixed, thank you.
Moreover, my service leaves room for the imagination,
which is something you have seldom thought
about, I'm sure. And secondly, my partnership
with morality is quite secure. Don't worry
on that score.

> *Nor am I puritanical, if that's what you are hinting.*
> *And as for imagination, why do you assume covering up*
> *does not reveal?*

Who started the morality crap?

> *You don't need to bite my head off.*
> *I have never been you,*
> *nor have you been me.*

Nor do I ever wish to be!

> *You love skin, admit it!*

Look who's talking!
Who envelops the largest organ?
Ironic that you covet what you hide
from others.

> *You are on dangerous territory, sister.*
> *What you hint, I am not.*

Touché.

> *F . . . f . . .*

Say it! Curse!

> *I was going to say Funny we should be talking about fabric*
> *when your owners are wiping us out! One-track mind!*

Ji . . .

> *Say it! Call me a jihadi!*

Who has a one-track mind?
I was going to say Jiminy Cricket! You're right!

> *I guess we are even.*

I guess so.

The Stuff of Scheherezade

I dream a poem and hold
a couple of words tight
to release onto paper.
Like Carla meeting
a stranger in Central Park.
They are on the same stone
bench overlooking the pond.

He turns to her and says
his wife saw him in a dream
and went all the way to India
to find him, wed him and bring
him to the United States.

Carla, who dwells in dreams
because they are more real
than being wide awake,
thinks, neat, you don't need a visa
to travel in dreams;
you can't fear being illegal,
deported, or jet-lagged.
She shakes her head,
not in disbelief but
in confirmation.

This man gazing at the pond
on this summer evening
flies back with his American wife,
before the INS wakes up
and shrugs at the long lines
awaiting the dull thud of endorsement
on crackling paper.

Between sips of tea, Carla tells me

it's not surprising his wife,
recently dead, visits him.
I see her traveling across death's checkpoint,
reaching out to Carla,
through her husband's waking exile
from oneiric enchantment.

Woman Poet

She is a balloon, rising, bumping against wood;
a cloud, changing and floating, lodging
in odd places, like a bathroom wall, under soles,
fingernails, she appears behind indifferent ears
like eggs magicians produce *Presto!*

Her words fill the afternoon, hesitantly,
like waves that do not fully crest
and roll up to waiting feet, but in her lines
she wades in blue streams, climbs mountains,
walks roughness like the wind, but when she
leaves her domain, her words flutter, then lie wrinkled –
thin skins that had stretched too much in joy.

Lover, baker, matchmaker, or more exotic,
a balloon woman to some, poet of things
marginal to living, like grammar or kite making.

Her form is ivory inlay that collects like frost
within the design, so you trace
the mahogany outline with your finger tip.

Draupadi's Dharma

Look around, dear Yudhishthira,
everywhere women yearn for the ordinary –
cook, clean, love, gossip, sleep –
dream ordinary dreams of years stretching out
like the view from a window,
trees against a blue sky, a road
with people beginning or ending their day,
birds pecking grain.

How long is this war?
How much longer, Yudhishthira?
I want a normal life in Hastinapura,
somewhere.

I want you to be a normal husband,
your brothers to live normal lives.
I've forgotten what normal feels like
among carnage wrought by willfulness.

You talk of grand things,
like getting your kingdom back,
but what of your dharma toward me,
your Draupadi? And love?

I want the simple,
the beginning when love created
the universe and the universe replied.
I do not want the poetry of incandescence,
exotic, grand truths, revelations.
I do not want to walk into a horizon lined
with fences of fire.

My spirit is resilient, no doubt,
despite my rape at that demon's wild hands,
your silence colder than death.
Listen, I'll be no pawn, no mute.
It's time for you to let go, Yudhishthira,
of your cock-eyed dharma;
I'm through.

Cartographer of the Breast

After the doctor saw the lump, a white bulb
in the gray moon of my mammogram,
the weeks, the wait in the clinic flipping
through Newsweek,
the needle, the star-like scar
turned in slow motion.

I floated into zero gravity,
my breast sampled for alien elements,
its results sorted under Latin names
and filed away in the belly of a computer.

Mother, nipple-less after the mastectomy,
father gently stroke-skimming
the air above the scar
to let her know he sees the flesh
that was, that fed their babies,
less perfect now,
but printed with memory.

She stays silent.
With craters so wide,
how to test the safe grounds
of conversation?

What can we say
about our role in the doctor's mission,
but carry the line
where the scalpel met the flesh?

And seas later
 – unlike the pain of birthing
where relief sings in your limbs –

we hope our feet meet earth.

Hunger Vigil

      for Narmada Bachau Andolan hunger strikers

We become shadows;
death reaches out
and we inch toward it,
our hunger like our cause
gnawing at the walls of logic
built around us,
calling the world to heed
our need to stand
on mother's shoulders.

If she submerges in the waters
of Narmada, our slow-crafted
peace talk will drown.

Where is the god you pray to –
the milk-and-*modak*-fed one?
Has he escaped again
to become the demon
who flings us away like chaff?

Old Narmada in our blood
will stave off death one more day;
her moonlit hair brushes past our faces.

Damn your calculating mind,
offering money that will cremate us
on non-existent land
your civilized tongue fabricates.
Now it is easy for you to
imagine our death, erase it
to flood your day

with a new water line, bank, sky,
our bodies, props for metal
and cement mountains.

The sun is hard today.
The crows gather, loud.

America's Collateral Damage

lately I don't want to be associated with America, I don't want to live on this soil, earn and spend here, everything I touch, the silks, the electronics smooth in my palm, the bills with their boxes for payment stuffed in crisp white envelopes, the evil shine of airports and government hallways, the fake courtesy rolling off of lips foreign to all but sale prices and holidays, oh, I don't want to live in a country perpetually at war with countries barely a tenth its size, I feel like the clowns in the White House and the Hill are speaking through me as I sit at the table and lift food to my mouth or bend down to read or chat with friends, their version of right and wrong, us and them has invaded my being and this virus is multiplying within me, it isolates me, incarcerates me, I am their collateral damage, and if I do escape elsewhere I will carry along this virus that harbors in me and it will continue to speak in other languages except the language of the soul, since prayer is alien to it, or compassion, or forgiveness, it is so oiled and fat with the proteins of its disgust, disbelief, and righteousness, it feels I am a fit vehicle for its travel, I am its true globalist, so I come back to my desk in my home in American suburbia and peel and peel away at the accumulated crud of malfeasance that has glued on to my basic commonsense values that made me feel human once, oh, am I nostalgic for that golden time when I was innocent and could tell war from peace, lies from truth, but now the exfoliation is probably going to be lifelong and become the karma I must battle in my next incarnation.

June Song

How one loves
this dark, steamy soil
one has stepped on
after a long time
the women have departed
with the rains
taking with them
the smell of fish
the sky is empty
a riot of ants
clamors on kitchen counters
a fly lands in
a drink
and stays there.

The Logic of Water

Post-Genesis Love

I was 15 when she kissed me on the mouth
and I did not turn away.

In moral science class my mind wanders
to her face so close to mine in that crowded
Calcutta Express where we said good-bye,
the gaggle of relatives going in and out
of her compartment arranging her suitcases
under the bottom bunk.

Sister Bee's stream of questions
on genesis and the commandments blurs
in the light of my love's face just there floating
above the Bible like a Mills and Boon romance
small enough to hide behind Mary the prostitute
at the feet of Jesus.

I kiss my beloved back and mango
branches rustle outside expecting rain,
the nun's voice flies into the sonorous dark,
her screeches blending into the train
whistling in my brain, distracting me
from perfecting the moment – harlequin lovers
in Bollywood-Radha-Krishna flamboyance
caught in a trance.

I look up to see the nun,
an enormous eagle, scaly wings
flung open, talons gripping the pages
that hold my love. I cannot decipher
the sharp cry – "you want
to be punished, child, do you, devil's
in you, child, you write an imposition
'I will never do it again,'" – it was
a wild tearing like an episiotomy
of the holy book.

The Logic of Water

I try other women's tricks,
light candles, smile at my husband
open a window to let the breeze

rhyme with Ravi Shankar's strings.

I ignore the anger. I try to hold on to
love wound tight around my finger,
frozen in the single diamond,
even though the serrated frame digs,
a gold barb.

Put the ring away.
Remember his tattoo on your skin –
indigo sky, a low moon,
a stream curling down
that band aids won't stanch?

I want to stay with this sudden
picture-perfect evening,
card games, popcorn, then
the blue flush of sleep
under a cloud of joined breath
long after video tapes end.

How do I shake off the shadows
that manacle me?

Remember   this is what
this is the way   this is how

One day I dream two sparrows show me
their home among maple branches.

A mysterious call to follow a web
carved by beaks and fall's adrenaline.

In the dusk of my dream
I see nests built and abandoned.
I speak of love
even as my romance lies
mangled.

Awakening, I speak love,
lifting a memory here,
a laugh there, an embrace.
Why seek delight?
Why hoard pleasure,
when flesh is peeled?

I peer deep into water.
Its light flows, unstoppable.

I meet the next wave,
my arms loving the weight
of water.

I Plant a Flag on My Tongue

1

Men veil and unveil you, bind your feet,
Sew your vagina, corset you till you're divided,
Wax, clip, fasten ribs with wire, bleach the wheat
Or olive of your skin, cut your boob, or pad it.
Pygmalions, they fashion you to their desire,
Chisel you to fit their gaze, and call it love.
Their works of art, you smile, granting their prayer
To remain faithful to lovers' whims; like doves,
You coo their glory and perpetuate on your bodies
Seen and unseen trauma. You name it "beauty."
Can you assert your dictated shape is your choice?
It's my body – you learn the jargon of individuality.
If only you'd ask skin and torso, ass and breast
Would they want to be free, they'll chant, "Oh, yes!"

2

When Ahalya's eyes strayed from her lord,
She was cursed to become a stone.
Metamorphosed into a rock's rough mold,
Her skin, her hair, & her sex became prone.
This inertness wasn't as new as people found:
She'd been taught to rest her gaze on feet,
Her husband's, god's, or her own, anklet-bound;
Watched, she kept within her husband's reach.
Long she heard through her stony undulations
Songs of poets, filling her with knowledge;
Warmth coursed through her rough grain,
Her limbs loosened into dance, and delight surged
Into every curve of her, willing her awaken
A world that had strayed from women.

3

Suturing lips excises the soul. Gyn-ectomy: Cut
The tongue that speaks pleasure
& sew the flaps tight to keep the secret
So safe, the heart doesn't stray. Not a tiny murmur
Will escape the fortress, think the custom police,
Long trained in the art of suppressing desire
& drafting the young into the Academy of Silence
To make boys goal-oriented and girls without ire.
When you hear women described as sharp-tongued,
Or condemned for having forked tongues, black
Tongues, spurned for being loose-lipped,
Or tongue-kissers, cheer, for they know the quick
Of speech, for silence is a tight-lipped war
Against us; only a free tongue is the winner.

Upping the Ante

"Fuck you!" she roared. "Now say it,"
she commanded. I tried to become large
like her, make every pore of my largeness
speak the words, blow things off my path.

I cursed repeatedly under the apple tree
in the artist colony, the green of New Hampshire
spreading around me, trying
to exhale the nasty horn of the 'f,'
digging deeper than "salah" or "paavi,"
tame Indian curses that didn't quite
tear open the fight in me.

She wanted me to engage with it,
beyond its casualness that made mothers
wash it out of my mouth with soap
and got teachers to make me swallow it
in detention rooms, or nuns to order me,
"Write 100 times, 'I will not say
Fuck you anymore,'" my unruly voice,
a viper among austere impositions.

So now in front of my new teacher
I disinterred my voice decibel by
decibel, knowing it would be years
of practicing like a devoted disciple
before I surprised myself, pronouncing
the curse, not letting it sag, stale.

Some image of things gone awry
jerked the words out of her,
straightening out her world.
The point was the apple in my hand,
her voice, my words.

Unholy Laws

My mother-in-law is visiting from Delhi,
a big place, to our little apartment in New York.
She shifts pots and pans to establish her way
among paper goods, trash can, microwave.
When she awakens, the clocks set their time,
rituals blaze in every cranny. From our balcony
above the pines flutters her holy sari in icy wind.
She is satisfied when a lock clicks into place.

My mother-in-law stops the new moon in its
orbit, starts it back on so it matches my period.
I am her guest three days of the month
when she places morsels three feet from my futon.
She believes that women should hide anger.
Cooking is our sole duty, it replaces sex
eventually.

Evenings we hold up the express line in King Kullen,
bags of cilantro and chayote on the counter,
the cashier's polished nails drumming steel,
while my mother-in-law chats with other mothers-
in-law from Madras, Bombay, Karachi.
She tells them she is doing her motherly duty
by visiting her son. To get back, God willing,
to one's own soil, to die in one's own cot!

Women Waiting

I don't want to be the woman at the window,
waiting, always waiting for a wing, a sign,
a ring.

I don't want to watch the road wind, imagine
the city beyond the cluster of trees, mist,
dust.

I don't want to trace loneliness in embroidery
thread weaving in and out of hankies, skins,
cushions.

I don't want to wait for the doorbell to announce
a husband, relatives, lost travelers,
passersby.

I don't want to study this pane, see my reflection
on winter afternoons, or in somber evening
light.

I don't want to write poems about waiting at a window,
my pen traveling miles, while I practice
rootedness.

Ghosts in My Ears

> *You must not tell anyone what I am about to tell you.*
> Maxine Hong Kingston, *The Woman Warrior*

As if spaces between stories
were quicksand
that will pull us in
and settle back
ripple-less

my mother skips details,
sketches enthusiastically
the parts we should hear.

So we flop around her
on our bellies
the cushions our boats
on the living room floor.

Like the time she tells
the tale of the serial killer.
How he disposed off the bodies.
Besides exaggerated descriptions
of the detective, a droll idiot
saved by coincidence,
we don't know if the victims
struggled, if they were women,
what was done to them.

Or the other story
of a girl losing her virginity
who then has her baby
and is clueless how it happened,
mother the raconteur is mum
to questions hitting us like meteors:
How? When? Where? Who knew?

And later, one cousin to another
How big was it?
Did you do it?
"It" reigns; body neutralized,
the self neutered,
when the unsaid rasps:
don't speak of It as we do
of eating, dreaming, pissing.

When sex is censored
my ears prick up.
I wait. Years pass.
I still don't hear.

But I know I have entered the silence of flesh.

I have to decipher its code,
speak of it on my own,
un-camouflage the body,
exorcise it,
shake out the whispers.

Cochin Tale

I hover on the edges of her story:
Mother by the front door, the ribbon of harbor,
framing father's anger leaping up in swathes.

I wish to huddle in her sari, fold my body in it,
the bulge of her pregnancy, an umbrella above me.
Stop! I yell at the swirling flames.

My feet are stone. There is no fairy
to draw out the silk of my world.
The distant ships unlock my heart.

The sea, the white sky pouring in
through windows, relentlessly,
sound out HOPE. Words pass

through her mind in two languages:
Naanam ille? Madhi, keto,
Have you no shame?
Enough, listen up,

and the subduing sound of the body
sinking, down, down.

These sounds burn a hole
I peer into on my dusty journey,
its dark blunting
memory's serrations.

Did she escape the fire,
the drunken creak of the door,
the windows lining up like guards?

Diminuendo

I had imagined the drama of my parents' separation:
suitcases stuffed with mother's saris, my dresses,
tattered Tamil magazines, silverware, and photos
lined up at the door; mother had sent the maid
to fetch the taxi. Soon we were on a train, speeding
to grandma's. At every episode, I changed the ending,

In each story mother had the last word,
while father sulked behind a locked door.
My future didn't lie in their litany of complaints,
but inhabited a world inked with my heart's hell.
I didn't know loss weighed like a gold coin
in the bottom of your chest. Nor had I seen
the battleground smeared with women's stories.
I lived in the dramatic moment, where vengeance
triumphed. Heroes and victims had definable faces.

Each time I pressed her to smash the invisible walls,
the treatises on femaleness became palpable in the air
we breathed – the letters rose up sternly, subduing
our bold eyes with their dazzle. One banner read *kadamai*,
duty, another read *nanri*, gratitude.

Mother sighed, you're right. But be a darling and
take the clothes to the laundry on your way to school.

First Bra Story

Well, there's the sports variety, tiny, sleeveless, scalloped vests,
with Winnie-the-Pooh gleaming brown and wholesome
like childhood,
at which my girl raises her eyebrows,
or Barbie smiling from a pink scooped neckline.

She turns away from the no-nonsense varieties
hanging demurely among flimsy polyester and cotton
to pick up long thin straps
supporting salmon padded cups on plastic hooks –
floating among stockings, panties, bikinis –
and holds them up for me to see a woman step into her.

Nice? she asks like the saleswoman
with shifty eyes in a dirty room in a store
years ago, and I had stood naked,
embarrassed at her raised eyebrows
at breasts on a nymphet, angry at those missiles,
now perhaps hills, bleached by garish lights,
exhibited on glass cases,
that threatened my landscape,
while mother waited at the counter examining prices,
readying her tongue for a good bargain.

I hook the eyelet and ask the image
with twin apples on the chest
in the long mirror
in a shuttered fitting room,
Comfortable?

Walls

He hands me small
and large pieces of the Berlin wall
wrapped in torn newspaper,
bits of German caught in jagged stone

as if to remind me of joy
catching in the nodes of separation.

In my purse I carry the pieces
still clinging to *freiheit* and *liebes-lieder*,
their cement smell mixing with powder
and a rouge-stained hanky.

Years later, I can't tell stone
from make-up,

the words are ash
and the debris can't be zipped up.

Killer Bees

Mother feels warm in this photo. Her hennaed fingers
the photographer has deliberately placed on father's hand.

Father sees her dark hair and glistening skin; his smugly
assessing eyes she ignores for a world whose joys she wishes
to pluck one by one and send them sailing into the air.

Did he sting her deep, did his poison carve in her
a black well? Or did she believe she could
pull out the sting, squeeze out the poison,
wedded life traceless of hurt?

In this photo, she is warm, rage bubbling
just beneath the skin. Twin pairs of eyes
focus, barely straying from instruction.

In the future, my wakefulness will demand
my sacrificial share. I am not yet born to tell
neighbors not to fall for her "unscarred bride" look
in the slim hands covered with gold, the large eyes
or father's smile and money.

In this photo they have not yet, not yet,
so neighbors can tell, "look what beautiful women do"
or exclaim, "the poor thing is mad" when her raving
reaches adjacent kitchens, or some cluck in sympathy
for father, "*Pavam*! Such a nice man!"

Thin

There they are, the thin women,
scattered around the room,
hollow-cheeked,
their eyes sparring with rouge-darkened skin.

Tight jeans and tanks bandage their slim
cookie-rod bodies that could break neatly in two.

Mina says her boyfriend pinched her torso
to measure her excess, trashed
her food and hung his tape measure,
a lasso, on their kitchen wall.
Unable to bear the watching numbers,
she camped in her bathroom, its walls
around her, thick, menacing.

I can't breathe, says Tara;
when I am on the scale,
my heart jumps. Last year
he thought my boobs were small,
so I stuffed silicone;
now my ass needs whittling.

Your story is like mine, another says,
my insides turn to ice,
my breath isn't mine.

Others witness multiples
of themselves mirrored in plush
middle-class ambience,

masking the smell of vomit
with *Obsession*.

My Body

This body browns into shadow,
glows when planets spin
around me.

I bend, lift, climb.
I swim in and out
of the engineering of do's and don'ts.

In giving and taking
I am neither he nor she, but
woman; my woes are of the womb
and the muscles of power;
my joys are of the womb
and the muscles of power.

Birds fly in and out of
the network of iron
built around me.

Soon fragments of prison
will lie among
my rich harvest.

Children of War

Mother:
> Abandoned child
> born of war in my body
> *don't be don't be*
> I am not your mother.

Born of men's thick rage
shadow child
clotted dark side of man
think why you came to be
then you will think of me.

Erase me.

You tore me as a final vengeance,
the enemy's last word
the key that will lock doors

even if it can open.

Child:

I am a child born of evil – a war
tore through my mother when I
saw light and pierced her with my cry.

I am a body that fights
to be to be to be to be
sheer will in the volume of sound
erupting from me.

In my dreams I hear her whisper:

erase me.

Mother:

Two enemies dwell in you
the powerful and the powerless
both brutal breeding a brute
two enemies you and you
soul and body love and hate
your body loves your body hates
your body remembers
your mother's rage.

Child:

I am a key that locks my door
that does not have a lock.
I don't know love
but I am a bird sitting on a branch.
Other birds join me and we live
together. It's fun.

But sometimes I wish for a hand
to smooth my forehead, drop
a kiss on it, as I once saw
in a movie in a camp.

I am a weed,
resilient.
I have sprouted feelings.
In my dream I learned love
when I saw a woman
smooth the forehead of a child
and drop a kiss on her head.

I am.

Lullaby

I gave her away
my one and only

I gave her away
when I was too young
to bring up a baby
all on my own
I gave her away
when society said

what were you thinking
when you had sex
would you have landed
with a degree instead

So I decided
to give her away

my body rocked

I was noisy
with pebbles in my soul

Years flew by

My baby became a girl
then a woman and a mom
She met me one day
it was as if
she never left my side

How could it be
I wondered then
Now I know
it's as simple as breath

I began quite early
to look at the world
with half-closed eyes
an oblique gaze –
philosophies tilted
and sky filled my shoes –
entered a dimension
few humans tread
located my baby
and drew her to me

I visited her daily
many, many years
traveling miles
without internet or wheels

In this other world
we spent magical hours
nourishing the cord
I thought I had cut
when I gave her away

So you see
when she is here
it's as if I've been her mom
all these many years
my image in her heart
and hers in mine
are the imprint of petals
pressed through the ages

My daughter I gave away
sits across from me
I never left she says
though you gave me away

Uncle's Letter to Father, 1980

you craved modern,
modern this, modern that,
wife showing skin,
twist, English, oatmeal, cake

now look where it's led you,
your running off to Bombay –
convent schools, your girl
going abroad alone,
I can understand if your boy
wants to head out,
but you're sending her to study in U.S.
as if there are no schools here

you could never control
your wife, and now look what's
happened with your daughter

tell her enough's enough
and get her married

what does she need higher
degrees for to wed
and have kids
she won't get any suitors
once she returns,
if you let her be a whore

worse, hook up with a foreigner
shame, is that what you want

don't write back

Dilli Ka Laddoo

Dilli ka laddoo, you describe my attitude,
my wish to possess my neighbor's life.

You say you get lonely, too, despite the man
in your life, the kids, the rituals rising like prayers.

Mother says if I marry and produce neat boys
and girls, all my problems will dissolve. . .

I wouldn't be lonely, she says, her voice crackling
across the Atlantic, "*Betiya*, let a man take care

of things and your burden will lift." I tell her
she's no psychic. She says, "But the Prophet is,"

drawing the wind out of my argument. I'm limp
as words from the Koran float up the Himalayas,

over the desert, across the Channel, and assert
themselves on my Boston telephone.

My womb dries up into a dust bag, the pods
that could've been Ayesha or Karim empty,

but my nipples flatten against my blouse,
my spine straightens, my chin lifts in defiance.

"Hai Allah," she will say, "there's no place
for women like you in Paradise."

Rhyme With Me

You have to look away
from Baghdad blushing
from sudden soft blooms
of whispered bombs
to campaign for metaphors
and hypnotize with rhyme,

as mothers in subterranean
spaces open up a page from Rumi
to soothe a child with visions of sunset,
of a man on a donkey sailing on the sand
to his beloved, the moon for company.

And the silence of her words
will fill the child's wracked bones,
despite atomic shudders,

as black Baghdad, painted by oil
and blood, a mural in rooms,
cafes, slums, ports and resorts,
drives your hunger for a Faiz,
an Akhmatova, a Darwish, to quell
the smoke billowing within,
opaque, velvet, unrelenting,

so emotion un-fleshed
is bearable, a crude comrade,
when you look away.

Women Like Us

Fragments of the Aftermath

1

she will not answer the door
she will not be evacuated
let the rain come she shouts
i'd rather wake up in heaven
than in some alien hell-hole

2

he summons the ghosts in his verse
in front of a noisy crowd in a dimly-
lit chicago café   i've seen too much
he says i can only offer you fragments
of suffering   his donation box fills up

3

this is america
these anguished
black faces are us
the president should have said
but he doesn't

the unspoken has settled
into our flesh   suffering
wears the same face on any soil

4

i'm now in school far away from the mississippi
    mom's back home tryin' to find a job i'm afraid to say
i'm unhappy my life sliced away so casually relatives chant
    thank god you're safe i'm supposed to feel lucky   grateful
i'm not supposed to feel guilty because i didn't do nothin' bad
    i hold words close to me like comfort mom doggy home cookin'
love

5

have all the dead been counted
which body is this arm attached to
how do you count dismemberment

the tally is deferred. . .

life goes on   the mayor is re-elected
by the living   plans for future
evacuations are made on dry land
under blue skies in the halo
of the disappeared

the city's comin' back say news anchors

the weather man spots unrest in the seas

one neighbor to another   do i rebuild
or become a refugee in my own country
there's nothin' for evacuees gawd i pay
my taxes   am I african or american

am I human

Peace

Peace is the trill of a child under fronds of summer,
the froth in the rim after you've drunk the day,
it is the sleep in your limbs after loving,
the gulls skittering over orange waves.
Peace is the shirt on a ravaged land,
the coolness of marble under your feet,
the taste of your lover tattooed on your tongue.

Peace is when children walk without fear,
when you comb out tangles from your hair,
when you chat with friends over tea,
when temples and mosques stand together like sisters,
when religion does not bloody streets, but balms sores,
when Allah and Vishnu are none other than breath in your body.
when men and women see the same energy beneath their skins.
Peace is the silence of god in the whorls of your fist.

Peace dwells in the geography of madness.
Hoard it under your pillow
and relish it in the stillness of dawn.

Mary at Chartres Cathedral

At Virgin Mary's shrine
I want to place my face
              in the folds of her dress

to cool my skin   hot
from the fiery outside.

Candles fence me from her.

So I stand on the gray stones,
gazing at her paleness against
the warm wood frame with its carvings
of flowers –

overlapping pointed petals
symmetrical like those painted or sculpted
in the temples of Durga or Saraswati.

Can this be the magical transfer of images
in migration?

              Physical travel in a past age?

And what of that other –
the spirit's trace of images through its
repeated births?

              Mary dreaming
of a Hindu goddess,

they dreaming me,

my heart lifting towards the holy.

Où Habitez-vous?

Where do you live, he asks in Tamil-accented
French. His wife in a red chiffon sari smiles.
Their children crane their necks
to look at the steeples of the cathedral,
their eyes screwed tight against the sun.
Seeing my blank look, he translates,

engirundu varel? I tell him, New York.
He says they've been exiles in France for ten years,
his family scattered all over Europe.

War rushes in and throws us around.
To regain play takes forgetting, or
a selective memory of joy.

I don't tell him I am not a refugee,
that I left home by choice.
I live in guilt; he smiles and moves on.

Nude

1

Space gives softness to her bend,
roundness to her breath;
It is the down above the lip.

Each of her horizons assumes magic;
where her shadow ends light begins.

Music breaks around the line,
a sea distant as a mellow heartbeat.

Listen to the shape of a woman filling
the center of this room.

2

Try matching flesh
with fresh paint:

The curve of the head, lashes,
a slice of chin, the pale
shadow of neck,
a round slab of shoulder,
the fat of the hip,
the crinkle in the waist,

the darkness where the legs meet
before one winds
its long way to the toes,
the other neatly folds.

The forlorn face reappears.

But where's the smile that passed
through her mind?

3

Snip some flesh from the waist
to match her accentuated slant.

Now the hands gripping the floor are young pines
and the rest, a gorgeous avenue.

Such loss, if my canvas cannot admit all of her.

Her hair, hands and feet
have to be imagined.
Not a footless goddess!

I want her to stand up and seize the colors,
catch the evasive.

4

On blue her muscles sing purple and green.
Yellows and pinks play in the shadows.

The painting ends
at the lips closed softly,
repressing her desire to speak.

You think she is vulnerable in her silence.
I think she is proud.

Either way, truth skims.
Both woman and artist.

5

He bends over his watercolor
of a woman reclining.
He fills her with flesh
except for her brown hair.
Blue waves lap around her.

He slides
a flat shadow onto her tall flank,
curving it into her crotch
as if to hush
the fierce reminder of light.
Her limbs are winter
as he bends over his palette
to dip his brush
trail a few more lines
quiet the feverish fragility
of pale pink.

He puts her away
when the lights dim
among bric-a-brac,
her lines tucked in his brain
one more step toward god
like a surgeon's cut
sure and fine
to prolong life.

Sex Contract

We don't want any surprises,
for they are sick or boring,
there are things we don't do,
you know what I mean,
and things we enjoy,

we don't have time for partners
to figure out your heaven,
so, honey, spell it out,
sign on the dotted line
so pleasure is primary;
it is your right.

Quit romantic notions of seduction,
don't keep your lover guessing,
stop counting stars to fill up conversation.

Knowing the other beyond this contract
interpreting bubbles of arousal,
walking into this theater
behind the screen of skin
is a bother.

Sign on the dotted line, honey, believe me,
despite the weight you give to mystery,
five kids later, kama drained
and sutra worn,
romance won't be your destiny.

Torque your illusions into revelation,
expose every nook of your erotic self,
sign on the dotted line, honey,
I swear, your soul will soar,
even if I don't believe in one.

The Escort

You can't go alone, you say.
Somehow, a companion
will give your words conviction.

When you say "he oppresses me"
you want the listener to feel these three words

the doer, the act, and the acted upon
etching themselves
matching each word

like fine rain, sharp, easy

as you have these last few years,
sleepless as you finger the welts
veiled even from you –

but you are afraid that after repeated telling
words become numb,
the nerves within them deadened,
cut off from the heart.

You think we travel as victim and victor,
oppressed and free,
but as you begin your tale again with hope,

a phrase knocks the wall around me,

your voice brings a shower of debris.

A Planet of Women

> *The feminist movement in Iran has branches in every home.*
> Shirin Ebadi, *talk sponsored by the Global Fund for Women, June 1, 2005.*

*When men go to war,
women stitch the hours, invent
stories to steady their hands.*

When the men don't return,
the women pick up the dropped stitches.

The metaphor unwinds
from its loosely looping skein.

I introduce my class
to women's struggles
in Muslim countries.

A slight, spiked-hair student says,
those women wear those *things*,
she gestures to her hair and face,
too disgusted to articulate –
hejab, burqua.
How can *they* be feminist?

Oh, to yank the veil covering
her sassy eyes!
My teacher voice says:
veil aside, what is the Iranian woman thinking
as she receives news of her husband's death
on the battlefield,
how does she get her child to smile,

what does she, who does she,
when, why, which, how,

what are her politics?

Images of behind-and-beyond-the-veil
women challenge my student's scorn
for Muslim women's concepts of love,
marriage, family.

I do not ask her:
do you protest, celebrate, advocate, burn?

I want to kick this cosmopolite out
of her gated haven.
I want to yell, the veil hardly hides
Muslim women's world;

their lives are filled with light and sorrow,
as are yours and mine,
unveiled though we are
and private we believe ourselves to be.

Afghan women ask
how can we carve our future
when death stalks us?

Veiled or not,
their question remains.

If death's an extreme case,
what's up with the French
banning head scarves?

I call a cease-fire
as I gather my books.

The afternoon brings
in its desert-pitch heat.

Next class I might open
a stubborn window.

Dancer

> *Splendid possibilities*
> *are open to us.*
> Anna Swir, *I Talk to My Body*

His hands fly up, crisscrossed,
a herring gull beginning to swoop
down, the nibs of his wing tips
fluffing air parting about his breast.

Arms out, he is geared
for landing, face kissing sky,
eyes rock.

When his plumes come down,
their slowness matches the violins
gliding low like love's invisible hand
tracing the belly's concave,
angle of knee,
perpendicular of spine:

This is the way the body moves –
out of itself into bird and animal –
leaning deeper into the world.

Mother's Weapon

My mother believed in the ritual of combing:
Each time she rubbed my scalp with jasmine-scented
coconut oil and ran her fingers through my tangles
before yanking handfuls of hair through a comb's wide teeth,

she believed she was a good mother like the other good
mothers all over India who pursued the same ritual
in mansion, rented house, shack, including the homeless
who found a dry spot by the giant waves of traffic;

how they pulled at the shiny black threads and braided tightly
their wish for long raven locks to attract handsome husbands
and looked into their daughters' dark, oily faces
free from the horrors of bad omens lurking
just outside the body that only the rhythm
of teeth against scalp could bar.

Listening to a Poet at The Frost Place, 1999

Her voice is a candle –

    it flickers,

        dips when words come heavy,

threatens to snuff out

    leaving a burnt wick of breath,

        inviting my nails

to nudge out freshly melted wax

    that was her voice.

Grandmother's Bedside

Come closer. Let me see those earrings.
Nice. You said your mother-in-law gave
them to you? She has good taste.
Sit comfortably on my bed. I don't
let anyone sit so close to grandma.
These bangles are heavy. Good to know
those jewelers haven't cheated.
Got to watch out, or those wretches
will sneak more copper into the gold.

I like how you painted me in blue silk,
hint of gold against my collarbone.
Makes me look taller than I am, masking
the 80 years bending me as if in revenge
for twisting to my will that trickster
fate that drives widows like me to choose
poverty or death. Anyway, enough about me.
Your mother, does she have the same maid,
the one with the crooked teeth?

And that cook, I heard you sent her away?
Good. Only connoisseurs know
the extraordinary. I'd rather cook
my own meal suited to my taste
than put up with shit that passes for food.

Kaikeyi to Her Husband

My wish killed you:

tricked by my stupor
in my darkened palace,
my rage tearing the terracotta
off the walls, my arrow-words,
"Exile Rama,"

you gifted me the joy
of seeing my son preempt
his older brother to the throne;

know I was selfish for my son,

(my concern so enormous,
it shadows the Kaikeyi you married,
the self-sacrificing one)

helping the weak, since the strong
can survive exile.

Night Vision

    for Sharmili and Laura

It is our last time together before
we fly in three different directions,
our pilfered store of jokes,
our armor,

when the Northern Lights surprise us.
We pull off the road to follow
the long glowing tails, giant strokes
moving from maple to oak
to pine, a pale, pale green
washing into silver.

This unexpected detour:
Wet mud hiding a wolf's paw
print, and above, a million stars.

Paradise in My Palm

Summer's a four-inch square wood piece
my daughter gives me as a solstice gift:
Cowries, a coconut, and an earthen pot
filled with liquid sun gleam in the shadow
of a palm tree. I imagine the sea folded
neatly around the slab's silver edges;
a woman steps from water, shaking
turquoise from her hair.

Why travel to the Bahamas when paradise
sits on a desk by your tablet, or at your bedside
by the reading light? You remember water
as you lift the colors, the smell
of salt, orange sand.

When frost lies like death on maple
brushing my window, I skinnydip
under a hot sun, steam rises from my skin
fogging the panes.

After a Guest's Departure

There's something about defining one's space,
proclaiming one's identity over a cooking range,
uninhabited by even a kettle, pots tucked away
into cabinets, *pulao* on the table's center,
violets dancing in the corner, empty counters,
and a refrigerator that could belong to a monk.

To be thin and spare, uncluttered with old news,
history stripped down to its barest details,
one thought going in and out like breath;
the enchantment of words worn like a habit
can keep the soul afloat, control its grammar.

Of what use are rituals of cooking, cleaning,
washing, drying, endless supplications to
water and fire, when the odor of staleness
robs the limbs of their limited energy,
ruins every joint and muscle of the spirit?
Even you don't know, you god of the seven hills.

You Don't Mind My Asking About Death, Do You?

My daughter asks me between bites of sandwich
where I would like to be cremated, here or in India.
I settled for the mother-daughter-daily-chat scenario,
but my dead body rears up between us.

"Here, of course." "Not India?" she asks, surprised.
"It's too complicated for you to cart my body across."
I don't tell her that dragging me through customs,
baggage claim, and taxi stands to the pyre
might leave her nightmares of bodies sitting up in flames.

"But it's so mechanical here – a few minutes
in a machine and you're ash." A leafless branch
scratches itself lazily on the window behind her.
"Exactly," I reply. "No mess. I like that."

Women Like Us

Ms. V, thanks for your class.
I learned more than I expected.
Like the first day you walk in,
I'm thinking, O God! No! Not an Indian.
I want to drop out.
I see you people on TV;
they stay in their saris
and speak with an accent that
makes me want out.
Don't get me wrong. I'm no racist
or anything like that.
But first times are crazy,
like falling in love or somethin',
if there's no spark, you get the hell out.
But I am glad, Ms. V, I stayed,
coz you knew stuff.
That first day sitting near the window,
and the screeching of them tires
makin' my nails dig into my thighs,
I tell my friends, let's leave.
But it's raining outside
and we don't have no umbrellas
and I don't want my make up to run,
and my hair cost a pile.
So I drag my ears to your voice.
You say about women, how we have
no rights and all, that we should speak up.
Enough with being silenced, you say,
and I turn to the faces next to me
and they nodding like this.
And this thought comes to my mind,
this lady ain't bad,
and I put Miss Costa in high school
in your place with her short hair,
tight skirts, and a tongue that sliced us

wafer-thin, and Miss Belinda calling
on just the boys, Mr. Evert
daring us into submission,
and you and all those other teachers
swim one into the other,
a reg'lar parade, Ms. V, and guess what,
somethin' goes off in my brain,
not my cell phone or pms;
it's that raw flame you talk about
that women like us burn with;
so, thanks.

Mother's Holidays

I knew when I came home from school
to a darkened house, that mother was reading
a novel, no time for chores, crass routine,
so the laundry smelled sour, plates waited
in the sink, the range stood empty, humid air
made the dust on the floor stick to our feet.

The crow had probably come that morning,
cawed himself hoarse for steaming rice
and had flown away disappointed. So too
the squirrel, the dove, and the sparrow,
ancestors low on the hierarchy.

Mother sat on the divan, her hair uncombed,
falling in curly waves to her hips, her sari
crumpled between her drawn up knees,
her bindi smudged, face unwashed.
Soon she stretched on the divan and held her book
toward the dimming light and read and read,
not getting up to eat, drink, or use the potty.

I would look up occasionally from my homework
to read her expression, a frown, a smile, mouth open,
sometimes pursed, face contorted, taut, or relaxed.
I could sense her breathlessness as she careened through
the juggernaut of emotions in another world,
climax, downfall, angst, revenge, forgiveness, reprieve.

She was unaware of us helping ourselves to leftovers,
doing our homework without our usual fights,
tip-toeing around our novel-reading mother,
disturb-proof glass separating her from us.
We learned how to wait patiently for two days,
sometimes three, until vexation gathered
like debt-collectors at the door, when
she finally emerged as if from a dream.

Me, Mama

*What's more important
than the book you lost*

      she asks, braces coating her smile,
shell-white behind dark waters

and I smile back, a minor tributary
      meeting a great river. She reminds me,
Your little girl, and I join her in chorus,
      tossing our joined waves cloud-high,
spray raining back on us,

      so this shifting memory remembers
this marker in my life – biological miracle
      turned eternal soul-stopping wonder –
that brims my banks.

Lake Woman

      Dedicated to Lake Superior

I dive into her icy, mossy depths
and come out numb, speechless.
Didn't I hear she is generous in giving speech,
not a thief of metaphors?

Yesterday she was so wild, I heard
every curse she screamed into the wind;
the gulls frozen on nearby rocks
flew up in terror. Today she pretends
it never happened; she serenely
lolls in her bath. Did I catch her wink?
The other day, she ate two boats,
yesterday she swallowed my friend's watch,
sparing my friend.

Tomorrow she will want my stories
despite the ones tucked into her ample
pockets, swelling like her veins.
I could run away from her, no regrets.
It'll be time anyway, when the moon hides.

But in my dreams, the fathoms
bid me enter her. She is a banshee
calling me to melt into her; only then,
she says, will I pour into words
that which slips from you quicker
than light, finer than sand.

Ghazal

Yesterday it drifted into my mind, heavy Calcutta rain,
a déjà vu, as I strained to see my way in the rain.

Roads, fields, playgrounds, school yards, the entire terrain
is a free-flowing river as we row to my aunt's in the rain.

I expect to see merely roofs when I approach her lane,
but I am greeted by windows and doors battered by rain.

Since the rooms lie submerged, I climb the drain-
pipe to see the vanished line between earth and rain.

Most families are perched on tables exchanging inane
jokes, playing cards and waiting for the end of the rain.

The thought of a watery grave can drive us insane.
But that is to be left unsaid, until after the rain.

Just as death holds life close like wood its grain,
so too does memory of dryness haunt rain.

Cars, huts, pots, pans, bodies, Muslim, Hindu, Jain,
turn up in every street in the hands of a marauding rain.

This is the fury unleashed on the Gangetic plain –
reminders of delusion by Kali's persistent rain.

How long do we remain under this awful reign?
I fear her words day and night between spasms of rain.

Listen, the goddess says, it's time to lift human pain,
so the earth once again reclaims ceded land from rain.

Notes

p.17 *Sita's Song*. "Kandeyn Kandeyn," a song by Sree Arunachalakavi, set to raga Vasantha, inspired this poem.

p.22 *A Sound's Body*. Assia Djebar's comment in the introduction to her book, *Women in Algiers in their Apartments*, that the Arabic word for "wound" also means "woman," prompted this poem.

p.33 *Draupadi's Dharma*. In the *Mahabharatha*, Draupadi, the wife of the five Pandava brothers who battle with their 100 Kaurava cousins to get their kingdom back, is pawned by her husband, Yudhishthira, in a game of dice he plays with the oldest cousin, Duryodana. When Yudhishthira loses the game, Duryodana disrobes Draupadi in public, but she is saved by the divine Krishna who miraculously keeps her clothed despite the yards of sari Duryodana pulls off of her.

p.36 *Hunger Vigil*. Narmada Bachau Andolan (Free Narmada Movement) is the largest movement currently in India to save the river Narmada and the indigenous people who subsist on it from the government's decision to build dams that will displace thousands.

p.65 *Dilli Ka Laddoo*. The last line was inspired by Nawal el-Saadawi's story, "No Place in Paradise."

p.86 *Kaikeyi to Her Husband*. In the *Ramayana*, Kaikeyi is the youngest wife of King Dasaratha. When she finds out that the oldest wife's son, Rama, was to succeed Dasaratha to the throne, she remembers a boon she had received from her husband years ago when she saved him from near death. She asks her husband to exile Rama and place her son, Bharatha, on the throne. Dasaratha is unable to back out of granting her wish and dies heartbroken at having to exile Rama. Kaikeyi is reviled by readers for her cunning; but this poem provides a different perspective.

About the Author

Pramila Venkateswaran, author of an earlier poetry collection, *Thirtha* (Yuganta Press, 2002), was a finalist for the Allen Ginsberg Poetry Award. She has published poetry in the United States, Canada, and India, in *Paterson Literary Review*, *Ariel: A Review of International English Literature*, *Atlanta Review*, *Prairie Schooner*, *Kavya Bharati*, *Long Island Quarterly*, *Calyx: Journal of Art and Literature by Women*, *Nassau Review*, and other print and electronic journals. Recent anthologies, *A Chorus for Peace*, *en(compass)*, *The Light of City and Sea*, *Long Island Sounds*, *Letters to the World*, and *After Shocks: The Poetry of Recovery* include her voice among poets from around the world. She has participated in multimedia presentations of her poems with dance, music and visual art and has performed her poems nationally, most recently in the Geraldine R. Dodge Poetry Festival. Her essays on race and gender have appeared in *Women's Studies Quarterly* and in *Language Crossings*. Her next book, *Wild Syllables*, is due shortly. She has a doctorate from George Washington University and teaches English and Women's Studies at Nassau Community College, New York.